THE WORLD'S
MINERAL
RESOURCES

Robin Kerrod

Wayland

First published in 1994 by
Wayland (Publishers) Limited
61 Western Road, Hove
East Sussex BN3 1JD, England

© Copyright 1994 Wayland (Publishers) Limited

British Library Cataloguing in Publication Data
Kerrod, Robin
    Mineral Resources. – (World's Resources Series)
    I. Title II. Series
    549

ISBN 0–7502–0884–8

Edited and typeset by Book Creation Services Ltd, London
Designed and illustrated by Talkback International Ltd, London
Printed and bound in Italy by G. Canale & C.S.p.a., Turin

Other titles in the series
The World's Energy Resources
The World's Food Resources
The World's Material Resources

Cover pictures (top to bottom) diamond mining, excavator, rubies, map of Australian mineral resources; (cut-out) selenite crystal.

The Maps: This book contains two kinds of maps: world maps which show the whole world (like the one below), and an area map, which shows only part of the world. The map below will help you to locate the region covered in the area map. The red box on this map outlines the area illustrated in the book on page 15.

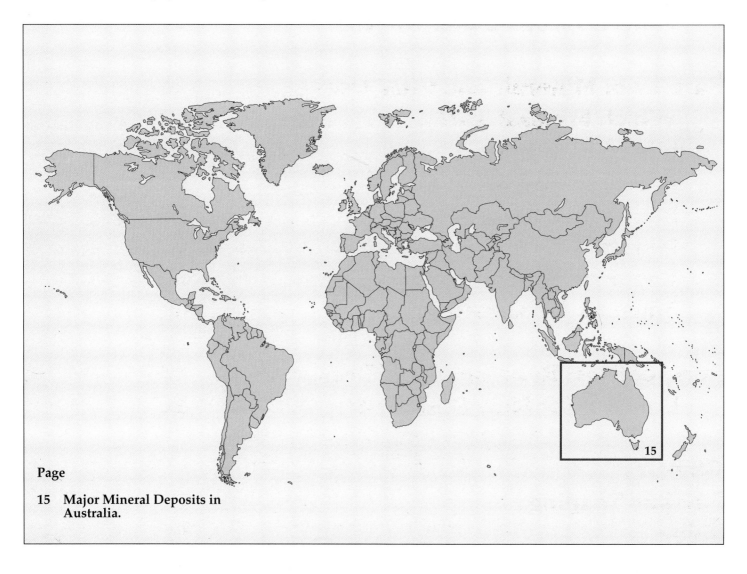

Page

15 Major Mineral Deposits in Australia.

CONTENTS

Introduction

The earth we live on is a huge ball composed of many kinds of rocks. The rocks are made up of chemical substances we call minerals. We mine, or take from the earth's crust, billions of tonnes of minerals every year.

Minerals are the most important of our raw materials. These are the basic substances from which we make metals, glass, chemicals, and other materials that manufacturers use to produce the goods we buy.

We also take from the ground vast quantities of oil, coal and natural gas. These are often called the mineral fuels. But they are also valuable as chemical raw materials.

However, the most valuable mineral resource for us and all living things is the liquid mineral we know as water. All living things need water to stay alive, and most industries need huge amounts of water to keep working. The water in the sea is also a valuable raw material, because it contains many dissolved minerals, including salt.

The air around us is an equally vital resource. It contains oxygen, which we and all living things must breathe to live. Air also provides important raw materials for industry.

The earth's mineral resources have taken hundreds of millions and sometimes even thousands of millions of years to form. It was once thought that these resources were so vast that they would last for ever. But we are now beginning to realize that we are using up some mineral resources so quickly that they could start to run out early next century. Understanding how to conserve or replace these resources is one of the most important problems facing the world today.

▶ Phosphates being loaded on to a tanker off the Pacific island of Nauru. Mining phosphates on Nauru is destroying the island, but has made the islanders rich. Phosphate deposits are used mainly for agricultural fertilizers.

PART ONE

Rocks, Minerals and Mining

Our planet is made up of three main kinds of rocks. These are called igneous, sedimentary and metamorphic rocks (see page 8). It was when such rocks were being created that many of the minerals we mine today were formed.

Some of the first mining was done by prehistoric people, who dug a kind of stone called flint from the ground many thousands of years ago. They used flint to make tools and weapons. By 4000 BC, people in the Middle East had discovered that some rocks – metal ores – could be converted to metal by heating (a process called smelting). One of the first metals produced by smelting was copper, which was used for making tools for the home, and weapons.

▶ Mining copper ore at Mount Morgan, Queensland, Australia, has created a huge artificial chasm in the earth.

Major Tin, Zinc and Aluminium Ore Producers

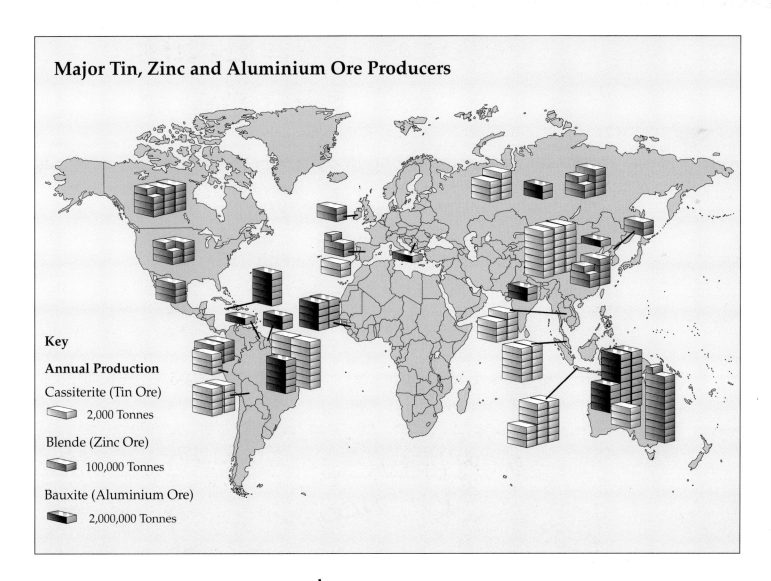

Key

Annual Production

Cassiterite (Tin Ore)

2,000 Tonnes

Blende (Zinc Ore)

100,000 Tonnes

Bauxite (Aluminium Ore)

2,000,000 Tonnes

Another useful ore contained tin. By smelting copper and tin ores together, early metalworkers produced the alloy (metal mixture) called bronze. Bronze was the first metal to be used widely, from about 3000 to 1500 BC, and because of this we call the period of history when it was used the Bronze Age.

By 1500 BC, iron ores were being mined and smelted, and the Iron Age began. Iron is the most important metal even today.

Copper, tin and iron ores are still mined in huge quantities, as are the ores of other metals, including aluminium. When miners have extracted all the minerals they can from the earth, they may turn their attention to outer space. Similar minerals are to be found on other rocky bodies in the solar system. We know this from the meteorites that have fallen to earth and from rock samples astronauts have brought back from the moon.

The Rocky Earth

The earth is a huge ball of rock with a diameter of 12,756 km around the Equator. Its north-south diameter, around the poles, is very slightly smaller: about 43 km less. The earth is surrounded by a layer of air, called the atmosphere, which is a few hundred kilometres thick.

The surface of the earth is partly land and partly water. The land areas make up only about 30 per cent of the earth's surface. The oceans cover the rest. The continents and the ocean basins form part of the hard outer layer, or crust, of the earth. The crust beneath the continents is about 40 km thick, but the crust under the ocean is only about one-quarter as thick.

Igneous rocks

Underneath the crust is a softer rock layer called the mantle. Sometimes this rock forces its way upwards in molten form through the crust. Often the molten rock, called magma, gets trapped below the surface and cools slowly there. But sometimes the magma surges up through the surface, pouring out as lava from volcanoes. As the lava meets the air or the water of the sea, it cools rapidly and becomes solid rock. Rocks formed from molten magma are called igneous ('fire-formed') rocks. Granite is an example.

Sedimentary rocks

Rocks on the surface are continually being worn away, or eroded, by the action of wind, rain, flowing water, ice and even plants. The rock fragments, such as sand and grit, are washed away by streams and are eventually deposited as layers of sediment. In time, the layers build up and get pressed together into solid rock. This kind of rock is called sedimentary rock. An example is sandstone.

Metamorphic rocks

The third main kind of rock, called metamorphic rock, forms when existing rocks are melted by heat and pressure inside the earth's crust. When they cool, their structure changes. Slate and marble are examples of metamorphic rocks.

▶ Molten lava from the earth's interior erupts from Kilauea volcano in Hawaii, USA.

Mineral Deposits

A few rocks are made up entirely of one mineral. Rock salt, for example, is made up entirely of the chemical called sodium chloride. Rocks like this, with a high concentration of one mineral, can be mined profitably as a mineral resource.

But usually rocks are not worth mining for their minerals. This is because most rocks are made up of a number of minerals, and these are scattered throughout the rock as small crystal specks, which are very difficult to separate.

It is usually only worth mining minerals when they occur as a concentrated mass, or deposit. Mineral deposits have accumulated in certain parts of the world because of processes that have occurred inside the earth's crust over many years. Some deposits form when molten rock, or magma, cools slowly beneath the surface. Heavy minerals containing iron and chromium tend to settle out first. The huge deposits of the iron ore called magnetite found in Kiruna, Sweden, were formed in this way.

▶ These white cliffs, the Old Harry Rocks at Studland, UK, are formed of chalky sediments that settled on the sea bed. Movements in the earth's crust then pushed up the sea bed over millions of years.

Just before magma finally sets solid, hot liquid solutions rich in minerals force their way into cracks in the surrounding rocks. There they crystallize, forming what are called veins, or lodes. Such deposits are among our most valuable sources of metals including copper, lead and gold.

Other mineral deposits form as a result of the action of the weather on rocks at the surface. The weathering process gradually breaks down the rocks, freeing the minerals they contain. Flowing water such as a stream carries the minerals away. The heavier minerals tend to sink to the bottom of the stream and, if there are enough of them, they build up into a kind of deposit we call a placer. Gold, silver and diamonds are often found in placer deposits formed this way.

Water may also dissolve minerals from the rocks it flows over and carry them away. Later, the minerals come out of solution to form a concentrated deposit. The great salt flats in Utah in the USA were formed like this.

▲ Kiruna mine, in Sweden, is one of the largest magnetite iron ore mines in the world.

◀ Salt can be produced by evaporating sea water in flat, shallow salt pans.

Where Mineral Deposits are Found

Mineral deposits are not found evenly distributed throughout the world. They are found only in certain regions where particular geological processes have been at work.

The most important minerals are the ores from which metals are obtained. Of these, iron, aluminium and copper ores are mined in the largest quantities.

Iron ores are much more widely distributed than the other ores, and they make about one-twentieth of the earth's crust.

Russia is the biggest iron-ore producer, with an annual output approaching 240 million tonnes. Brazil, with about 200 million tonnes, and Australia, with about 110 million tonnes, are the next biggest. The USA, Canada and China are also leading producers.

Large deposits of copper ores are found near the Pacific coasts of North and South America, in Chile, Peru, Mexico, the USA and Canada. Chile produces the most ore - over 1.8 million tonnes a year.

▼ At Kennecott Bingham Canyon mine in Utah, USA, huge trains are used to carry copper ore away for processing.

PROSPECTING FROM SPACE

Because the world is using up minerals so quickly, mining geologists spend a great deal of time and money looking for new deposits. They use space satellites to pinpoint likely areas for exploration. Remote-sensing satellites, such as Landsat, **SPOT** and **ERS**, take pictures of the surface in light of different colours (or wavelengths). The images they send back, such as this Landsat photograph of central Utah, USA, can reveal surface detail that is invisible in ordinary photographs.

In addition to the other American producers, there is an important 'copper belt' in Africa, with both Zambia and Zaire being major producers.

Aluminium is the most plentiful metal in the earth's crust. But the only useful aluminium ore so far discovered is bauxite, which contains the aluminium compound alumina. Unfortunately, workable deposits of bauxite are much less common than those of copper and iron ores. Australia and Guinea produce the most bauxite. Brazil, Jamaica and Surinam are also major producers.

Copper and nickel are sometimes extracted from the same ores. For example, the ore in the major copper region of Sudbury, Ontario, Canada, is also rich in nickel. And Canada is one of the world's leading nickel-mining countries, producing over 200,000 tonnes a year.

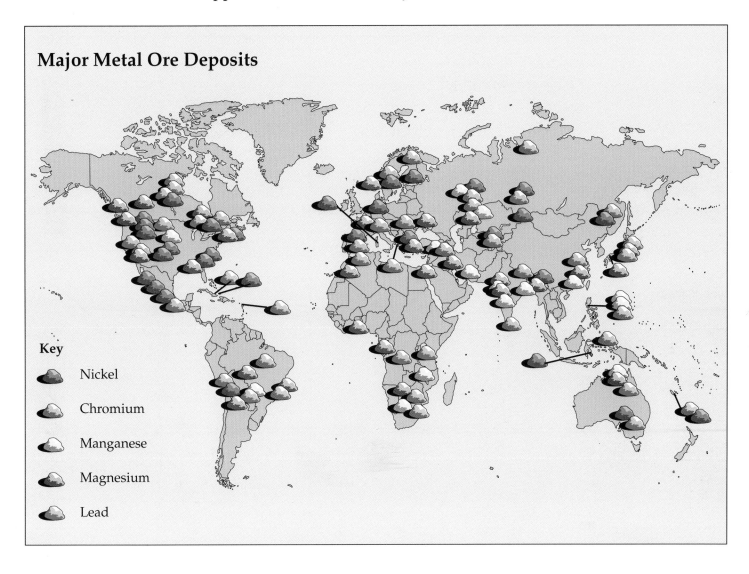

Major Metal Ore Deposits

Key
- Nickel
- Chromium
- Manganese
- Magnesium
- Lead

Mining Surface Deposits

Mineral deposits that occur on the surface of the ground are quite easy to extract. Fortunately, many important ore deposits do occur near the surface. Bauxite is mined in this way, and so is much iron ore, copper ore and coal.

At its simplest, surface mining consists of digging out the mineral deposit from the ground and loading it into trucks or railway wagons for removal. This mining method is called opencast or open-pit mining.

▼ At Port Hedland, Australia, massive mechanical excavators are used to move large quantities of ore.

PANNING FOR GOLD

The prospectors in the famous 'Gold Rushes' in California, Canada and Australia last century worked the placer deposits in stream beds. They used to 'pan for gold', as this Brazilian is doing, above. Panners would gather a pan full of gravel and swirl it round with water. This would wash away light materials and leave behind heavy specks of gold – if they were lucky! The same principle is still used today in panning for gold on a commercial scale. Stream gravel is washed into a series of 'sluice boxes', and any gold settles out in grooves at the bottom.

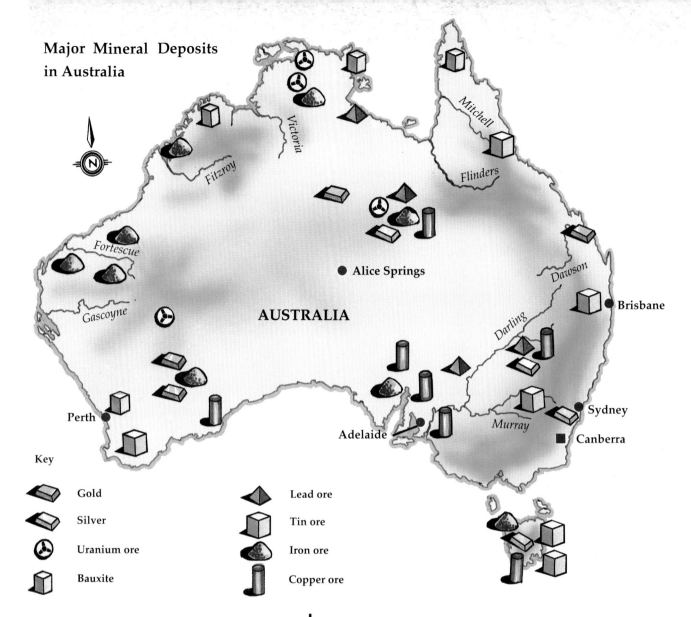

Major Mineral Deposits in Australia

Key

- Gold
- Silver
- Uranium ore
- Bauxite
- Lead ore
- Tin ore
- Iron ore
- Copper ore

Most deposits are covered with a layer of soil, which is called the overburden. Huge excavators, such as draglines and bucket-wheel excavators, are used to strip away this soil. Then power shovels dig out the ore. If the deposit is hard, it can be broken up with explosives before removal.

Mining placers

Placers are deposits of heavy minerals that have been deposited by flowing water. Gold may occur in small quantities in placers, and some prospectors search for it by hand using a technique known as 'panning' (see box opposite).

The tin ore called cassiterite also occurs in placers, and these are found in great quantities off the coast of Malaysia, in South-east Asia. These placers are worked by huge floating dredgers, which can process up to 15,000 tonnes of ore-rich gravel a day.

Mining Underground Deposits

Many valuable mineral deposits occur in veins running through the rocks deep underground. Coal, gold, silver, copper, nickel, lead and zinc ores are among the minerals mined underground.

To mine them, shafts are sunk into the ground, and tunnels are dug out to reach the mineral vein. The miners use explosives to bring down the rock face and break up the ore. They drill holes ('shot holes') in the rock and explode charges in the holes. The shattered rock is then taken to the surface.

Coal is usually mined underground using powerful cutting machines. This method is possible with coal because it is so much softer than most minerals.

As mining proceeds, shafts and tunnels are extended to reach new parts of the mineral vein. In some mines, tunnels run for hundreds of kilometres on various levels.

BORING METHODS

Some underground mineral deposits are mined from the surface. Crude oil is reached by drilling a deep bore hole. The drilling rods (left) have spiral channels through which drilling mud is circulated to flush out rock chippings.

Salt can be obtained by 'borehole mining'. Water is pumped down a borehole into an underground rock salt deposit, where it dissolves the salt. Then the salt solution is pumped out and the salt is recovered by evaporating the water. In the USA underground deposits of sulphur are extracted by a borehole method called the Frasch process. Superheated water is pumped down the borehole to melt the sulphur. Then compressed air is blown down and forces the molten sulphur to the surface.

▲ A vein of gold shows up clearly in a Brazilian mine.

Underground mining is more expensive than surface mining, and much more dangerous for the miners. For safety, the shafts and tunnels are lined and supported as protection against falling rocks and from cave-ins. Ventilation equipment must be installed to keep the miners supplied with fresh air and to prevent a build-up of dust and poisonous or explosive gases, such as 'firedamp', or methane.

In deep mines, air must be refrigerated to keep it cool. In the Western Deep Levels mine at Carletonville, South Africa, gold is being mined at a record depth of nearly 4 km. At this depth the temperature is over 50 °C; in contrast, ordinary room temperature is about 21 °C.

How a Coal Mine Works

A rotary coal cutter (1) moves along the face of the coal seam and deposits coal on to an armoured conveyor belt (2). It is then transferred on to the main conveyor which loads it in to the coal skip (3). The coal is raised to the surface by a lift mechanism (4) before going on to a washing and sorting plant (5). From here it is loaded on to trains for delivery.

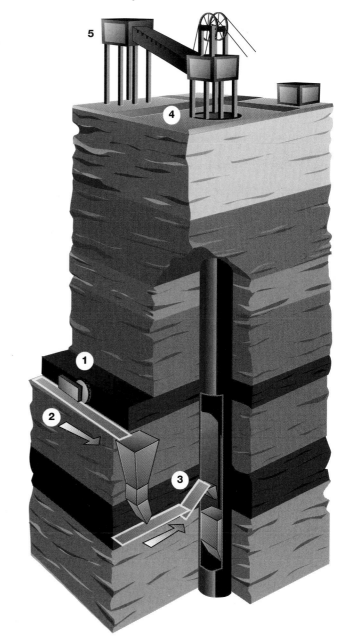

Water Resources

Water is a vital resource, essential to life on earth. Every living thing contains water and must have water to live. More than two-thirds of the human body is water. The water in the blood carries dissolved substances, such as sugar, to every cell in the body.

Fortunately for us, and for all other living things, there is plenty of water on earth. Over 70 per cent of the earth's surface is covered with the water of the oceans. The oceans contain 97 per cent of all the water there is. Half of the remaining water is locked up in the ice caps at the Poles. The other half is found in rivers and lakes, or in the ground: this is the freshwater we depend on to stay alive.

On average, people in developed countries each use about 250 litres of water a day. They only drink about two litres, and use the rest for flushing toilets, washing, cleaning cars, and so on. In countries affected by drought, however, people have barely enough water to drink and cook with each day.

Industries often use huge amounts of water. An electric power station may use 250 million litres of cooling water every hour!

The freshwater that is available to us is constantly being used up and then replenished by rainfall in an important natural cycle – the

THE WATER CYCLE

Water escapes from the surface of the earth all the time in the form of vapour. It evaporates from oceans, lakes, rivers and the soil. Plants give off water vapour too in a process called transpiration. The vapour rises into the air and cools. This makes it condense, or form water droplets, which we see as clouds. When the droplets are big enough, they fall as rain (or snow if the temperature is below freezing). Then the cycle begins again. Each day, over 1,000 cubic kilometres of water evaporate from the earth. An equal amount returns, mainly as rain.

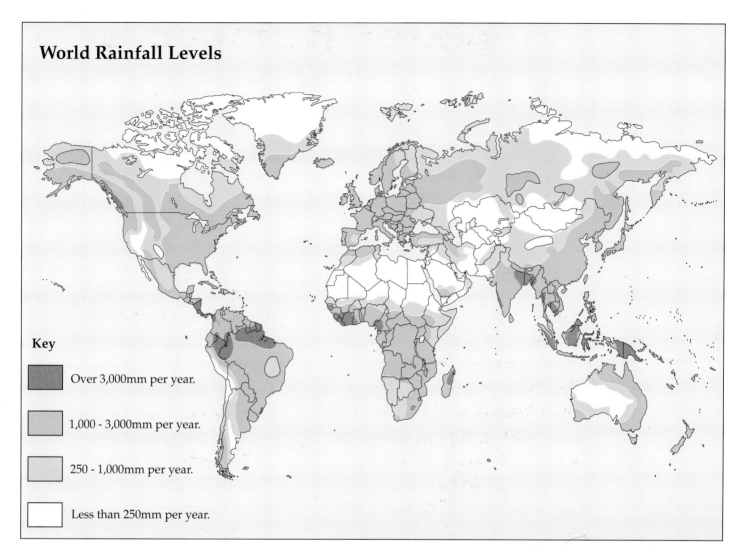

World Rainfall Levels

Key

Over 3,000mm per year.

1,000 - 3,000mm per year.

250 - 1,000mm per year.

Less than 250mm per year.

water cycle. Unfortunately, rain does not fall evenly over the earth, or equally throughout the year. Regions in the tropics may have up to 2 m of rainfall each year, while desert regions may be lucky to have 2 cm. In the Atacama Desert, in Chile, it has hardly rained at all for 400 years.

▶ Icebergs and the polar ice caps hold about half the world's freshwater.

Minerals from the Sea

The rivers that flow over the earth's rocks gradually dissolve many of the minerals they contain. Eventually the rivers run into the oceans, carrying the dissolved minerals with them.

Over millions of years, the oceans have become a storehouse of dissolved minerals, or salts. The most plentiful salt in seawater is sodium chloride, which is also called common salt.

Seawater is one of the major sources of this salt for industry. Most other chemical elements are present in seawater to a greater or lesser extent.

In the oceans as a whole, the total amount of some minerals seems enormous – there are some 60,000 tonnes of gold, for example. But it is so thinly distributed that it would be very expensive to extract. The same is true for most of the other elements, except for magnesium and bromine.

Tapping the oceans

Common salt, sodium chloride, is easy to extract from the sea. In hot

► This desalination plant in Nevada, USA, is beside Lake Mead, which is an artificial lake formed by damming the Colorado river.

▲ Rock salt is usually mined from caves, not very deep underground.

countries, the sea is run into shallow coastal basins, where the heat from the sun evaporates the water, leaving the salt behind.

Magnesium can be extracted from magnesium chloride – a compound present in seawater. The seawater is mixed with slaked lime (calcium hydroxide) so that the magnesium is precipitated (comes out of solution) as magnesium hydroxide. This is then processed further to produce magnesium metal.

Bromine is extracted from seawater by another process. The water is first made slightly acid and then treated with chlorine. This converts the bromine atoms in seawater into bromine gas, which is removed by a current of air. Further processes then concentrate the bromine. Very large volumes of seawater have to be processed because bromine is present in such small amounts – only about 70 parts per million.

The sea is also a source of iodine, an element closely related to bromine. It is not extracted from the sea itself, but from seaweed. Some seaweeds absorb and concentrate the iodine, which can be extracted from the ash remaining when the seaweed is burned.

▼ Nodules of manganese, mixed with other metals such as copper and cobalt, have been discovered on the seabed. Unfortunately, they occur at such great depths that it is difficult and expensive to collect them.

The Air

The air about us is, like water, essential for keeping all living things alive.

The Composition of Air

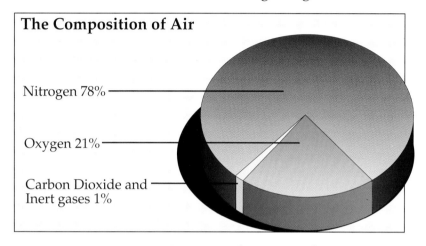

Nitrogen 78%

Oxygen 21%

Carbon Dioxide and Inert gases 1%

Air provides us with oxygen to breathe. Oxygen is absorbed by our lungs and passes into the blood to be circulated to all the cells in the body. The oxygen is used to 'burn' food to provide us with energy. Without a continuous supply of oxygen, the cells would quickly die.

Air is a mixture of gases. Oxygen makes up about 21 per cent of the air by volume. Most of the rest (78 per cent) is nitrogen. Argon makes another part (0.9 per cent). It is one of the inert or 'noble' gases, so called because they do not normally react with other chemicals. Other noble gases, such as neon, krypton and xenon, are present in the air in tiny amounts.

Carbon dioxide is present in air in small quantities (0.03 per cent). This gas is produced when food is

▶ At a temperature of -195 °C nitrogen is a liquid. The 'steam' in this photograph is water vapour that has condensed from the surrounding air, because of the cold.

▶ The Space Shuttle main engines burn a mixture of oxygen and hydrogen - which are stored in the engines in liquid form.

burned inside our bodies, and is released into the air when we breathe out. Carbon dioxide is also produced when anything containing carbon burns in air. Plants use it to make their food. But too much carbon dioxide in the atmosphere can be harmful, because it acts like a greenhouse to keep in the earth's heat, and so contributes to global warming (see page 45).

Raw materials

The air provides industry with raw materials. Nitrogen is used in the manufacture of ammonia, which is made into fertilizers for agriculture. Industry also uses liquid nitrogen (with a temperature of $-195\,°C$) for cooling purposes.

Oxygen is the 'hidden' chemical involved in any chemical process that involves burning. Liquid oxygen is used as a rocket propellant – the space shuttle burns more than 600 tonnes of liquid oxygen every time it blasts into orbit.

A major use for the noble gases is in electric discharge tubes, such as neon lamps. Argon is used, with nitrogen, to fill light bulbs.

Minerals from Outer Space

▶ This crater in the Arizona desert was formed by a meteorite that landed there 25,000 years ago.

Iron was first smelted from its ores in about 1500 BC, yet iron beads and ornaments have been found in tombs in the Middle East dating back nearly 1,500 years earlier. How could this be?

The reason is that iron used before 1500 BC did not originate on earth. Thousands of years ago, people found lumps of pure iron that had come from outer space.

The earth is continually being bombarded with particles from outer space called meteoroids. In fact it gains about 5 million tonnes in weight from such particles every year. Mostly, meteoroids are tiny and burn up in the atmosphere, creating streaks of light we call meteors. But some are much larger, and survive their fiery journey through the atmosphere to reach the ground, as meteorites.

If the meteorites are really big, they gouge out huge craters in the ground. A huge meteorite smashed into the Arizona Desert in the USA in prehistoric times and blasted out a crater 1,265 m across and 175 m deep (see opposite). It can be seen there today, well preserved by the desert climate.

Some meteorites are stony, being made up of fine-grained rock like basalt. Some are iron, being made up of a mixture, or alloy, of iron and nickel. Other meteorites are stony-iron, being a mixture of rock and metal.

Meteorites are not a practical source of minerals for industry, but they are important to geologists and astronomers, because they show that matter in outer space is similar to that on earth. This was confirmed when the US astronauts journeyed to the moon in the 1960s and early 1970s and explored its surface. They brought back 385 kg of rocks and soil samples. The minerals found in the samples were very similar to minerals found on earth. But one new mineral was found. It was called armalcolite, after the names of the astronauts – Armstrong, Aldrin and Collins – who were the first people to set foot on the moon, in 1969.

▼ Astronaut Harrison Schmitt collected rocks from the moon during the USA's Apollo 17 mission in 1972.

PART TWO

Minerals and their Uses

▶ Quartz crystals come in many colours - from clear to smoky brown. But the basic shape of a quartz crystal is always the same (see page 31).

▼ Micro-circuits can be formed in tiny chips of silicon crystal, as small as the head of a needle.

There are about 2,000 kinds of minerals in the earth's crust, but only about 30 are common in the surface rocks. They are sometimes called rock-forming minerals, and include quartz, feldspars, calcite, gypsum and pyrites. Quartz is the commonest mineral of all. It is found in the form of beautiful transparent crystals in granite rocks and also as specks of sand on the seashore.

Quartz is the common name for the chemical silicon dioxide (also called silica), a compound of silicon and oxygen. Most of the minerals in the earth's crust are oxides, silicates, carbonates, sulphates or sulphides combined with other elements, typically metals.

When metals are extracted from their ores, the process usually involves separating them from the metal oxide, sulphide, carbonate, sulphate or silicate. Although minerals are valued mainly for the metals they contain, some have uses themselves, in pure or combined form. Silica, for example, is used to make glass. Malachite, a form of copper carbonate, is a green-coloured stone used for decorative purposes. Corundum, a common form of aluminium oxide, is used as an abrasive for grinding. Ruby is a form of corundum prized as a gem.

The uses of the metals extracted from mineral ores are so varied that it is hard to imagine life without them. Modern buildings, transport vehicles, telecommunications equipment, cooking utensils, and nearly all industrial machinery depend on a wide variety of different metals for their shape and function. And perhaps the most useful mineral of all in our modern age is oil, used for fuel or for making plastics.

▼ The White Sands National Monument, in New Mexico, USA, is a vast area of wind-blown white gypsum, the chemical calcium sulphate.

Which Mineral is it?

Manufacturers use different minerals to make the thousands of products we use in our everyday lives. Each of these minerals has special properties that make it suitable for a particular use. Each also has certain characteristics that enable geologists to identify it when they are prospecting, or looking, for a new source. Let us look at some of these characteristics.

The first clue to identifying a mineral is colour. For example, the bright green of malachite is easy to spot. But colour can be deceptive. The golden-yellow colour of iron pyrites is easily mistaken for that of gold; hence the mineral's common name, 'fool's gold'.

A mineral's density provides another clue: some feel much heavier than others. Barytes, which can look like calcite, feels much heavier when held in the hand; its common name is 'heavy spar'.

The mineral's lustre, or the way it reflects light, is another useful way of identifying it; many ores have a typical metallic lustre.

The hardness of a mineral is also unvarying. It is measured on the Mohs hardness scale, which rates the soft mineral talc (as in talcum powder) as 1 and the hardest mineral, diamond, as 10.

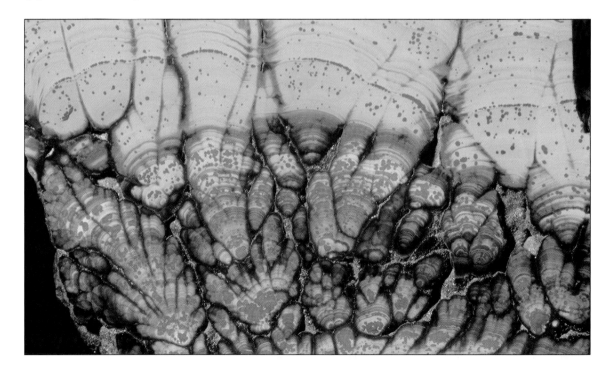

▶ Malachite, a beautifully textured green stone, is a form of copper carbonate.

◀ Veins of pure gold are often found in quartz.

The shape of a mineral's crystals and the way the crystals split, or cleave, are other useful identifying properties. So is the colour, or streak, the mineral might leave on the surface of a white tile.

Taken alone, none of these characteristics will define a particular mineral absolutely. But taken together, they can help to identify it beyond reasonable doubt.

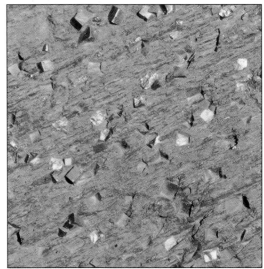

◀ It is easy to confuse pure gold with shiny iron pyrites, shown here, which is more common and less valuable and so is known as 'fool's gold'.

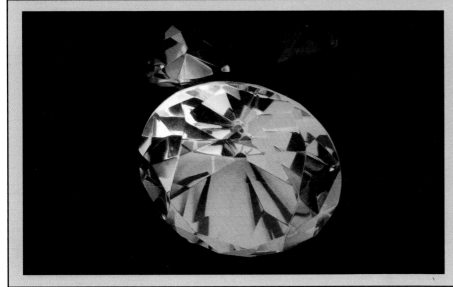

MOHS HARDNESS SCALE

A scale of hardness for minerals was devised by the German mineralogist Friedrich Mohs in 1812. It lists 10 minerals in order of hardness, from the softest, talc, at 1 on the scale, to the hardest, diamond (left), at 10. On the scale, a mineral will scratch ones below it and be scratched by the ones above.

10	Diamond	5	Apatite
9	Corundum	4	Fluorspar
8	Topaz	3	Calcite
7	Quartz	2	Gypsum
6	Feldspar	1	Talc (softest)

Mineral Crystals

When you look closely at a rock such as granite, you can see that it is made up of tiny coloured glassy bits. These are mineral crystals. In the granite, the crystals are all jumbled up and have no particular shape. They all grew together in a dense mass when the rock was formed.

Sometimes, however, mineral crystals form in cavities in the rocks, where they are able to grow without hindrance. As a result, they grow into a characteristic shape and can become quite large.

Wherever the same mineral is allowed to grow unhindered, it grows into the same crystal shape. Rock salt – the mineral from which we get our table salt – always crystallizes in little cubes. So do fluorspar and the lead ore called galena. On the other hand, the common mineral calcite, the main ingredient of chalk and limestone, forms clusters of long, six-sided 'fingers' tipped with little pyramids. This form of the mineral is often called 'dog-tooth' calcite because of its appearance. Quartz forms similarly shaped crystals.

▶ Basalt is a rock made up of countless tiny crystals. They can be seen as colourful fragments when a thin slice of the rock is viewed through a powerful microscope in polarized light.

The space lattice

The external shape of a crystal is determined by the shape of the basic structure of the mineral. We call this basic structure the space lattice. The atoms that make up the mineral are always arranged in the space lattice in the same positions.

Rock salt, for example, is the chemical compound sodium chloride. Each basic particle is made up of a sodium atom combined with a chlorine atom. In the rock salt space lattice, the sodium and chlorine atoms are arranged alternately in a pattern of cubes, so the crystal also has a cubic shape.

There are six basic ways in which atoms arrange themselves in crystals, and these give rise to different 'families' of shapes. For example, some crystals are long and thin, but square in cross-section; others are six-sided, or hexagonal; others are long and rectangular in cross-section, like a plank of wood; and still others seem to lean to one side.

▲ Some minerals form regular crystalline shapes. A good example is selenite, which has formed into the mass of regular crystals shown above.

Precious Stones

▲ Rubies are transparent crystals of aluminium oxide (corundum). Traces of chromium oxide give the crystals their red colour. Natural rubies are valuable gemstones, but rubies can also be produced artificially.

The colour and sparkle in the most beautiful jewellery are provided by precious stones, usually called gems or gemstones. They are normally set in precious metals such as gold and platinum. The finest gems are prized because they are beautiful and rare. They are also hard, which means that they are not easily scratched or damaged and therefore keep their appearance as time goes by.

The most valued gems include diamond, emerald, ruby, sapphire, aquamarine and zircon.

More common and less hard are semi-precious stones, such as amethyst, which is an attractive violet form of quartz.

All the gems mentioned so far are crystals. However, the shapes of gems in jewellery are not the natural shapes of the crystals, but shapes into which they have been cut or polished. Typically, gems are cut with numerous flat faces, or facets, so that they reflect light and sparkle or shine. But some are cut with a rounded surface, which is called 'cabachon'.

Some gems, such as turquoise and lapis lazuli, are not crystals, but are opaque stones. Another stone that seems opaque because it reflects light from its surface is opal, which shimmers with ever-changing patterns of colour.

The big four

Diamond is the most prized gem and also the hardest. Its hardness comes from its very strong crystal structure. It is a rare form of the element carbon. Australia and Botswana are leading diamond producers. Poor quality diamond, called bort, is a valuable industrial abrasive, or grinding agent.

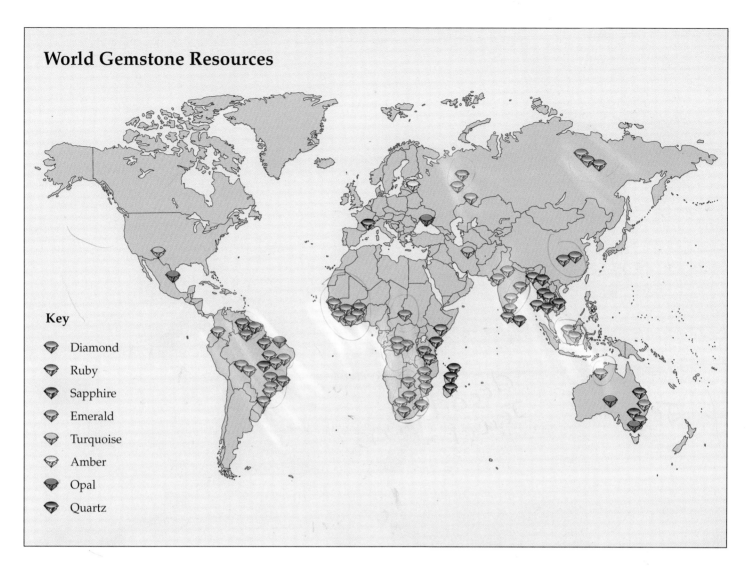

World Gemstone Resources

Key

- Diamond
- Ruby
- Sapphire
- Emerald
- Turquoise
- Amber
- Opal
- Quartz

Emerald is a rare green form of the mineral beryl, whose chemical name is beryllium aluminium silicate. Sapphire (blue) and ruby (red) are different forms of the mineral corundum (aluminium oxide). Some of the finest emeralds come from Colombia, while some of the best sapphires and rubies come from Burma and Thailand. Synthetic ruby is produced commercially, for example to make the crystal rod for ruby lasers.

◄ Precious stones such as diamonds are prized as decorative jewels for their rarity and beauty. This woman is from Rajasthan in northern India.

33

Minerals for Metals

Over three-quarters of the chemical elements that make up the earth's crust are metals. But only a few of them can be found in metal form in the ground. We call these native metals. They include gold, silver and platinum, three of the most precious metals. These metals are found native because they do not react readily with most chemicals. For example, the only acid that will dissolve gold and platinum is 'aqua regia', or 'royal water', a mixture of concentrated hydrochloric and nitric acids.

The majority of metals are too reactive to be found native. They are found combined chemically with other elements in minerals. When these minerals form concentrated deposits that can be profitably extracted and processed into metals, they are called ores. The most common method of processing ores is smelting, which involves heating the ore in a furnace with other materials.

Many ores are oxides, chemical compounds in which the metal element is combined with oxygen. The iron ores magnetite and haematite are oxides. So are cassiterite (tin ore) and bauxite (aluminium ore). Sulphide ores are also common, and in these the

▶ Some mineral ores form curious shapes when they crystallize. An example is haematite, a form of iron ore called 'kidney ore' because of its rounded appearance. This piece comes from Cumbria, UK.

metal is combined with sulphur. Galena (lead ore) and blende (zinc ore) are both sulphides.

Copper is extracted from ores of many kinds. Chalcopyrite is a sulphide ore containing iron as well as copper; cuprite is a copper oxide; and brilliant blue azurite and green malachite are both copper carbonates.

Sometimes an ore can be processed directly in the form in which it comes from the ground. The iron ore magnetite is an example of an ore with a high concentration of metal.

Most ores contain only small amounts of metal, commonly only a few per cent by weight. Before it is practical to extract the metal, the ore must be concentrated and the large quantity of waste matter (known as gangue) has to be removed. Methods of doing this are known as mineral dressing.

One of the most effective methods is froth flotation. This method of mineral extraction is used in processing copper, zinc, lead and nickel ores. The ore is crushed fine then treated with chemicals before being added to a bath of frothy liquid. The chemical treatment makes the fine metal particles attach themselves to the bubbles in the froth, while the unwanted particles sink to the bottom. The froth can then be skimmed off.

Minerals for Chemicals

Many other minerals apart from metal ores are valuable. Some are useful in their basic form.

One example is asbestos, a mineral that occurs in the form of thin fibres that are heat-proof and fire-proof. Most asbestos is produced from a mineral called chrysotile, and is used for making heat-proof textiles and insulation. Asbestos can cause serious lung diseases, so must be used with extreme care.

Other valuable minerals include pure-white kaolin, or china clay, the main ingredient in fine pottery and porcelain. Limestone is a vital raw material for several industries.

It is used, for example, in the blast furnaces that make iron. Limestone is also used in glass-making, with another common material, sand.

Pure white gypsum, which looks like chalk, is used to make plaster of Paris, which sets hard when mixed with water. Hospitals use plaster of Paris to make the plaster casts that help fix broken limbs.

Common salt – which as a mineral is known as rock salt or halite – is the starting point for producing several valuable chemicals, including caustic soda and chlorine. These substances are produced by the electrolysis of a strong salt solution, or brine. Electrolysis involves passing electricity through the brine, in order to separate the elements. Caustic soda (sodium hydroxide) is a cleansing agent and an important industrial chemical. Chlorine is used as a bleach, for sterilizing swimming pools, and for making many products, including refrigerants, pesticides and plastics.

Graphite is a native form of carbon, chemically the same as diamond but the atoms are arranged in a much weaker structure. Hence graphite is one of the softest of all

▶ Safety suits made from asbestos are used by fire fighters to protect them from the flames.

Major Phosphate and Sulphur Deposits

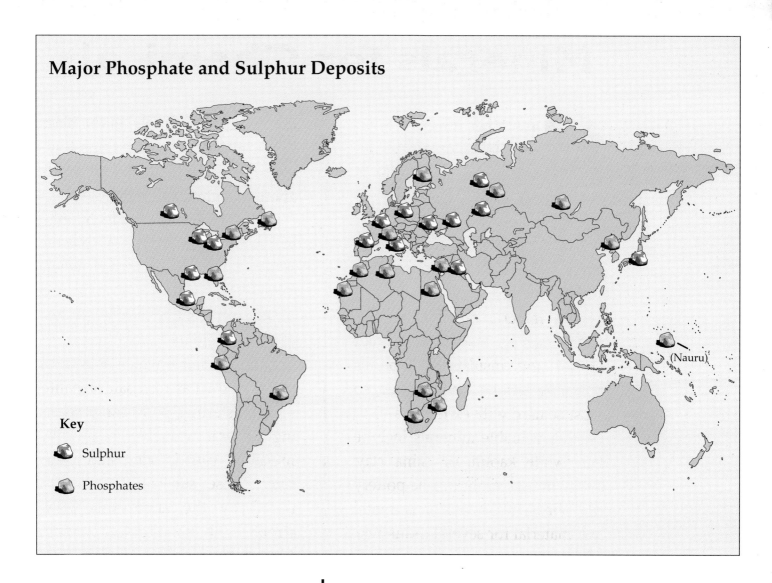

(Nauru)

Key

🪨 Sulphur

🪨 Phosphates

minerals. Pencil leads are made from graphite.

Sulphur is another native element, often found in volcanic regions. It is one of the most important of all industrial raw materials because it is made into sulphuric acid, used in a wide range of manufacturing processes. It the USA, vast sulphur deposits are found in structures called salt domes along the coast of the Gulf of Mexico. The sulphur is taken from the salt domes by borehole mining (see page 16). In other countries sulphur is extracted from pyrite, or iron pyrites. Spain is the country with the largest pyrite deposits.

Phosphates are also extremely important, especially for their use as fertilizers. Combining sulphuric acid with mineral phosphate produces the fertilizer called 'superphosphate'. The USA is the largest producer and user of phosphates.

Petrochemicals

Crude oil, or petroleum, has become the industrial world's most important source of energy. From it we get the petrol, kerosene, diesel fuel and heating oil we burn in our cars, planes, and furnaces.

But in many respects, burning oil to produce energy is a waste because crude oil is a storehouse of valuable chemicals. From these chemicals we can make plastics, paints, synthetic fibres, dyes, explosives, drugs, pesticides, and a host of other products. We call the chemicals we extract from oil petrochemicals.

Crude oil is a mixture of literally thousands of different chemicals called hydrocarbons, which are made up of hydrogen and carbon only. The molecules, or basic units of these chemicals, are built up on a 'backbone' of carbon atoms, linked together in chains or rings. Carbon is the only chemical element that can link with itself in this way.

Crude oil is processed into useful products in an oil refinery. The first refinery process is distillation, or fractionation, which splits up the oil into a number of parts, or fractions (such as petrol, kerosene, and others) according to their boiling points.

The heavy oil fractions, which have the highest boiling points, are not useful as they are. But they can be converted into more useful,

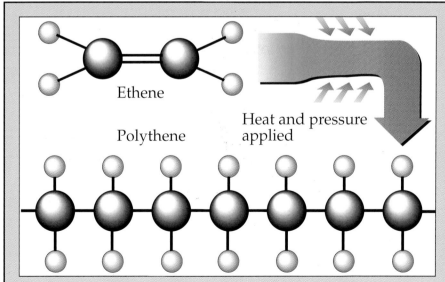

Ethene

Polythene

Heat and pressure applied

BUILDING UP PLASTICS

Plastics are produced from petrochemicals by a process called polymerization. This is a process in which substances with short molecules (monomers) are built up into substances with long molecules (polymers). For example, the starting point for the common plastic polythene is a gas called ethene, produced during petroleum refining. At high temperature and pressure, the gas polymerizes: its molecules join together to form long chains, and the result is polythene.

lighter oil fractions by a chemical process called cracking. Cracking breaks down the large molecules in heavy oil into the smaller ones found in petrol, for example.

Cracking also produces a variety of other liquid hydrocarbons useful as solvents – liquids that dissolve other substances. Gases are produced as well, and these can be processed further by polymerization. Polymerization is the opposite process to cracking: it joins up small molecules into bigger ones.

An oil refinery produces hundreds of different products from the chemical 'cocktail' that is petroleum. Not a bit of it is wasted. Even the thick, sticky tar left over at the end of processing has a use, as the bitumen that is mixed with crushed stone to make tarmac for road surfaces.

▲ Here you can see the energy released by a burning oil well in Kuwait. Engines and furnaces of all kinds are designed to use the energy released when oil burns.

Minerals for Construction

People have used the mineral materials around them to construct dwellings, temples and monuments ever since the dawn of civilization. Some bricks made of mud, found in the ruins of the ancient city of Jericho, in the Middle East, date back to nearly 7000 BC. Today, people still build with sun-dried mud bricks in some parts of the world. In the Americas these bricks are called adobe.

Where available, stone was the preferred building material for major building works. The Great Pyramid at Giza, in Egypt, was built with more than 2 million limestone blocks weighing up to 2 tonnes each. The construction of the pyramids is still considered to be one of humankind's most remarkable building feats.

The great construction engineers of the classical world were the

▼ The Egyptian pyramids were built with huge limestone blocks. The pyramid in this picture was finished around 2465 BC.

▲ Cement is made in factories such as this one in Greece.

Romans, who left a legacy of fine buildings, bridges, aqueducts and roads. They used stone with great skill, and they also introduced a form of concrete, which is now the most valuable material for the modern construction engineer.

Modern concrete is made by mixing together cement, crushed stone, gravel and sand. These last three materials are extracted from the ground in vast quantities, probably more than 50 billion tonnes a year worldwide. Crushed stone, gravel and sand are used not only for concrete, but also for the foundations of roads.

The commonest form of cement is called Portland cement because the concrete it produces looks like grey Portland stone. The cement is made from clay, chalk or lime-stone, and often other mineral materials, such as iron ore and gypsum. The ingredients are baked at a temperature of about 1,400 °C in a rotating furnace, or kiln. The hard mass of 'clinker' that results is then ground into the familiar fine cement powder.

Modern civil engineering works, such as dams or bridges, use vast amounts of concrete. One of the most massive concrete structures ever built is the Grand Coulee Dam in Washington State, USA. Completed in 1942, it is made up of over 8 million cubic metres of concrete and holds back the water by its weight of 20 million tonnes.

▼ The simplest bricks are made of mud formed into shapes and left to harden in the sun .

Running out of Resources

Every year it is estimated that some 50 thousand million tonnes of minerals, rock, gravel and sand are dug, ripped or blasted from the ground in mining and quarrying operations. This can have a devastating effect on the landscape.

Opencast mines are particularly destructive, laying waste huge areas of land that will never recover their original form. For example, the Fortuna-Garsdorf opencast coal mine near Bergheim, Germany, covers more than 20 square kilometres, excavated to a depth of more than 250 m.

Opencast mines and quarries are often a source of dust pollution that can blanket the surrounding landscape. Even when the mines are underground, the surface is often covered with huge heaps of spoil, or waste material. These spoil heaps can be dangerous, and sometimes slip like an avalanche, burying everything in their path. It was such a slip that caused the Aberfan disaster in South Wales in 1966, in which 116 children and 28 adults died when a school was buried.

Minerals tomorrow

We are using up our mineral resources very rapidly, and early next century many existing mines will be exhausted. This will mean that mining geologists will have to find alternative sites for mines, which will put even greater pressure on the environment.

Geologists calculate when supplies of a particular mineral might run out by dividing the estimated reserves of the mineral by the annual rate at which the world uses it. The reserves are the amounts of the mineral they think can be extracted from known deposits.

▼ Modern industry uses large amounts of water, and also often pollutes its sources, such as this lake.

▼◄ Diamonds are usually mined deep underground (below) but in Namibia (left) they are found on the surface. They are collected by massive mobile sifters, which unfortunately also damage the surface irretrievably.

Among the minerals most under threat are the ores of gold, silver, tin, lead, zinc, copper and cadmium, supplies of which may be exhausted by the middle of next century. Among other minerals, supplies of diamond, asbestos and sulphur will also not last longer than a few decades.

By contrast, there are enough deposits of the ores of iron and aluminium, the world's commonest metals, to last for three to four centuries at present rates of usage.

But the signs are that one of our most vital minerals, crude oil, or petroleum, will start to run out

next century. This will cut off the supply of petrochemicals, the starting point for plastics and many other manufactured materials.

Looking for New Resources

It will no doubt one day become economical to extract some of the very scarce minerals from seawater, in which they occur in very low concentrations. Extracting some minerals from the deep seabed may also become economically worthwhile. Manganese nodules, which contain copper, nickel and cobalt as well as manganese, are found widely in the oceans, but at depths of 3 km or more. At present this makes it almost as difficult to mine them economically as to mine minerals in outer space.

Mining outer space

In the longer term, it is possible that geologists will have to extend their activities to outer space to acquire vital minerals. The moon has been shown to have much the same kind of minerals as our own planet, so this could become a possible source for them.

Far-sighted prospectors have suggested that we look even further afield for minerals – to the thousands of rocky bodies to be found in the so-called asteroid belt, between the orbits of the planets Mars and Jupiter.

Coal tar

If supplies of petroleum run out in the twenty-first century, industry may have to turn to coal tar to produce petrochemicals. Coal tar, obtained by 'distilling' coal, was the original source of carbon-based chemicals.

Our most vital resources

Modern industry has put our vital resources of water and air under considerable threat. This is partly because it is using more and more of the world's freshwater resources for industrial processing and for cooling purposes. By doing this, industry is reducing the amount of freshwater that is available for drinking, cooking and other uses.

▼ Industrial towns, such as this one on the Yangtze river in China, can do enormous damage to the environment if the pollution they produce is not controlled.

In all parts of the world, rivers, lakes and the sea are being polluted by factory wastes, which often contain poisonous products. The air is being polluted by fumes from factory chimneys and motor vehicles, which affect people's health and cause acid rain.

The build-up in the atmosphere of gases such as carbon dioxide (which is produced when engines or furnaces burn oil or coal) is contributing to global warming. This could bring about changes in climate that could raise sea levels and also turn large areas of the earth into deserts. Other chemical pollutants are damaging the ozone layer high in the atmosphere, which helps protect us from harmful rays from space.

It is becoming clear that we must take action now to protect our two vital global mineral resources – water and air – if we are to avoid permanent damage to our world.

▼ The increased amount of carbon dioxide and other gases in the atmosphere acts like a greenhouse, keeping in more of the sun's heat, and causing global warming.

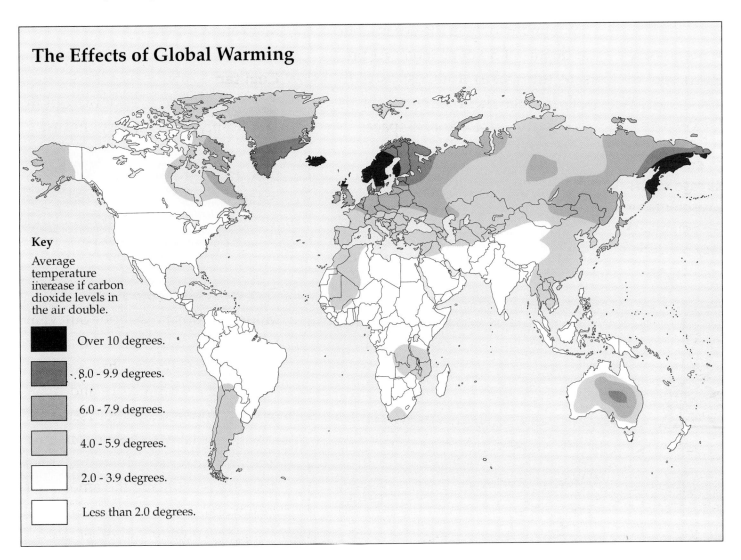

The Effects of Global Warming

Key

Average temperature increase if carbon dioxide levels in the air double.

- Over 10 degrees.
- 8.0 - 9.9 degrees.
- 6.0 - 7.9 degrees.
- 4.0 - 5.9 degrees.
- 2.0 - 3.9 degrees.
- Less than 2.0 degrees.

GLOSSARY

Atom The smallest part of a substance that can exist. Atoms are very tiny: one hundred million atoms side by side would measure only one centimetre.

Compound A substance made up of two or more chemical elements combined together.

Core The central part of the earth, thought to be made up mainly of the metals iron and nickel.

Cracking A process used in oil refining, which breaks down heavy oils into more useful lighter ones.

Crust The relatively hard outer layer of the earth.

Crystals The regular shapes many minerals take when they form. The same mineral always forms the same shaped crystals.

Electrolysis Splitting up a compound into its elements by means of electricity.

Elements The basic chemical 'building blocks' that make up matter.

Gem A precious stone, such as diamond and ruby.

Geology The scientific study of the earth and its surface.

Global warming The gradual increase in the temperature of the world being brought about by the build-up of certain gases in the atmosphere, including carbon dioxide.

Igneous rock Rock formed when molten magma from the earth's interior cools on the surface or underground.

Magma Molten rock in the earth's crust, which sometimes thrusts its way to the surface, in volcanoes.

Mantle The part of the earth between the crust and the core. It consists of rocks that are partly molten.

Metamorphic rock New rock formed when existing rock (igneous or sedimentary) is changed by heat and pressure in the earth's crust.

Meteorite A rock from outer space that falls to the earth.

Mineral A chemical substance found in the earth's crust. Most minerals are compounds containing two or more chemical elements.

Mineral dressing The process of preparing mineral ores for smelting into metals.

Native element An element that can be found in its pure state in the earth's crust. Gold and carbon are examples.

Opencast The method of mining minerals on the surface.

Ore A mineral containing a metal, from which the metal can profitably be extracted.

Panning A simple mining technique used by gold miners. They swirl a mixture of gravel and water round and round in a pan. Any gold present settles out.

Petrochemicals Chemicals obtained from petroleum, or crude oil.

Petroleum Oil found underground in the rocks. It is called 'crude oil' before it is refined.

Placer A deposit of a heavy mineral, such as gold, found typically in a stream bed.

Plastics Synthetic materials that can be readily moulded into shape. They are made by polymerization.

Pollution The poisoning of the land, the water, the air, and the environment in general.

Polymerization A chemical process in which a substance with small molecules is changed into a substance with large ones.

Precious stones Minerals prized because of their beauty and rarity, such as diamond, sapphire, emerald and ruby.

Refining Purifying or converting a substance (such as metal or petroleum) into a more useful form.

Rock The solid part of the earth's crust. Rocks may be made up of a single mineral, but are more usually made up of several minerals mixed together.

Sedimentary rock Rock formed out of layers of sediment on the sea bed or on a river bed. The sediment may be broken-up bits of old rock or chemicals that were once dissolved in water.

Smelting Heating metal ores fiercely in a furnace so as to extract the metal.

Space lattice The shape in which the basic particles of a mineral are arranged in a crystal. It is responsible for the external shape of the crystal.

Synthetic Made wholly from chemicals; not natural.

Water cycle The never-ending process in which water is exchanged between the earth's surface and the atmosphere.

Further Reading

Baines, J *Water* (Wayland, 1991)
Conserving Our World series (Wayland)
Dixon, D *The Big Book of the Earth* (Hamlyn, 1991)
Focus on Resources series (Wayland)
Kerrod, R *Raw Materials* (Wayland, 1990)
Leggett, J *Air Scare* (Heinemann, 1991)
O'Donoghue *Rocks and Minerals of the World* (Dragon's World, 1993)
Parker, P *Water for Life* (Simon & Schuster, 1990)
Pellant, C *Rocks and Minerals* (Salamander, 1990)
Resources Today series (Gloucester Press)

Picture Acknowledgements

The publishers would like to thank the following for supplying photographs: J Allan Cash Picture Library, cover cut-out, pages 6, 9, 12 left, 23, 24, 27, 31, 34, and 41 bottom; Frank Spooner Pictures, page 5, 39; Hutchison Library, title page, page 43 top; Science Photo Library, cover bottom, pages 12 right, 16, 20, 21 bottom, 22, 25, 26 top, 28, 29 middle, 30, 32, and 36; South American Pictures, page 35; Wayland Picture Library, cover top, pages 11 bottom, 19, 21 top, 26 bottom, 41 top, 42, 43 bottom, and 44; Zefa, cover middle, pages 10, 11 top, 14 both, 17, 29 top and bottom, 32, 33, and 40.

INDEX